SEQUOYAH REGIONAL LIBRARY
3 8749 0064 40283

FUN·TO·LEARN

SIZES

Claire Llewellyn

Consultant: Dr. Naima Browne

LORENZ BOOKS

NOTES

Fun to Learn Sizes introduces children to the concept of size. Lively pictures and stimulating activities encourage them to understand and compare the differences between sizes.

Learning the basics

This book shows children that size is one of the ways in which we group things. Matching, sorting and classifying are important concepts. They are behind the mathematics covered in the first year of school.

Reading together

You can help your child by reading aloud the words that accompany the pictures. Go through the book at your child's pace, looking at each concept—one at a time. Allow plenty of time to talk about the ideas before moving on to the next one. Make reading time fun and enjoyable.

Talking it through

Help your child's understanding by encouraging them to talk about the pictures and relate what they see to their own experiences. This will help your child to develop self-confidence and make the ideas more tangible.

Learning by doing

Encourage your child to try the activities. They can help to extend and develop skills further. Try to make everyday activities an adventure in learning—cleaning their room or going to the supermarket offer plenty of opportunities to talk about size.

Checking your child's understanding

Check your child's understanding of size by asking useful questions about everyday activities. For example, when you are setting the table for a meal you could ask—Which spoon is the biggest? Which glasses are the same size?

CONTENTS

What size are you?

Tall, short, little, big—all of us have the same shape, but we come in many different sizes.

I can stretch myself out wide.

I can hold myself in until I'm as thin as a pin.

Who is taller? You, or your friend? Take off your shoes, stand back-to-back, and see who is taller.

This huge teddy bear is bigger than me.

This little teddy bear is smaller than me.

My legs don't
stretch very
far yet.
My legs
are longer.
I have the
longest legs
of all three.
When you do a
forward roll . . .
you go from tall . . .
to a small, tight ball.
Stretch up tall . . .
bend your knees . . .
crouch down . . .
and tuck in your head.
Is your hair . . .
. . . short, . . .
. . . long, . . .
. . . or in between?

Bigger and smaller than

Look around you each day and find people, places and things that are bigger or smaller than each other.

An Afghan dog is much bigger than . . .

a Yorkshire terrier

enormous present

smaller present

My small lollipop will soon be gone.

big rabbit ears

smaller cat's ears

My bigger lollipop will last all day long.

The small fish is after the big shark's tail.
Uh-oh!
My big shopping bag is too heavy to lift.
My small handbag is light to carry.
Would you prefer a big bunch of flowers . . .
or a pretty little posy?
You are much smaller than the fire-breathing dragon.
RUN!
These beads are small. I can hold dozens of them in my hands.
These beads are smaller. I can hold hundreds of them in my hands.
Have you heard the story of Pinocchio?
His nose grew bigger . . .
. . . and bigger . . .
every time he told a lie.

Small, smaller, smallest

We sort small things in order of size: small, smaller and the smallest of them all.

small ladybug

smaller ladybug

smallest ladybug

Small peas always seem to taste the sweetest.

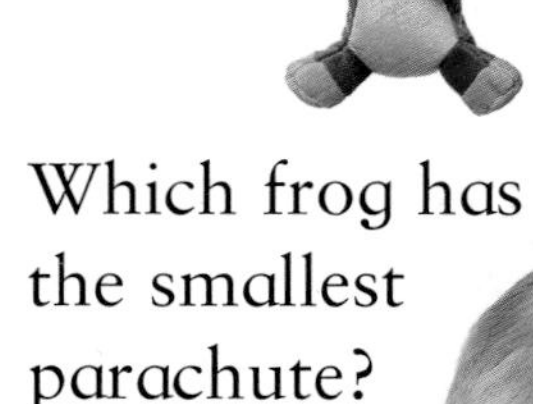

Which frog has the smallest parachute?

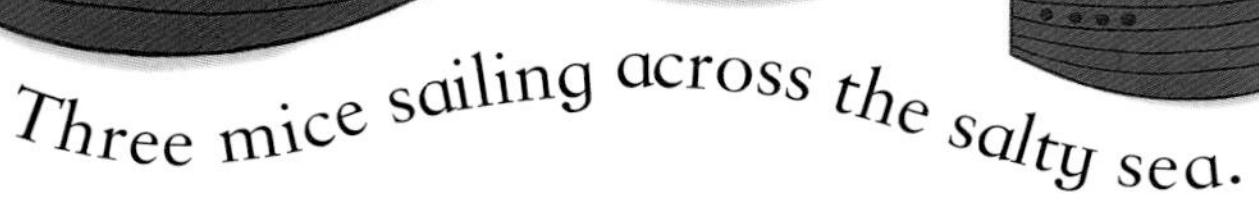

Three mice sailing across the salty sea.

Small fish swimming, one, two, three.

Try this!

Make cookies in three-sizes

1. Buy some ready-made cookie dough. Find three cutters of different sizes.

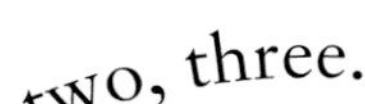

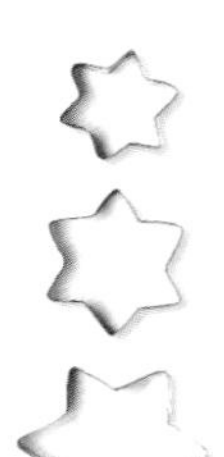

2. Roll the dough flat with a rolling pin.

3. Cut out the cookies with the three cutters.

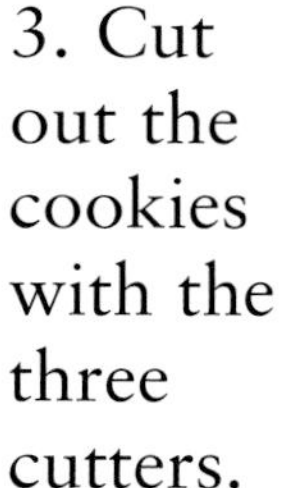

4. Bake until they are golden brown.

Can you sort these hats in order of size?

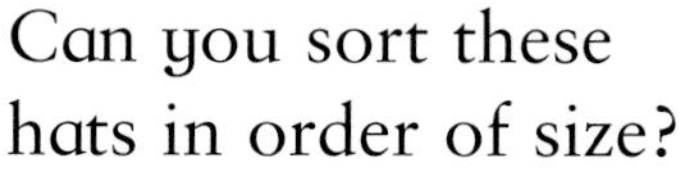

Big, bigger, biggest

Find the **biggest** ballerina . . .

Long and short

Can you sort long things from short things? Look at the objects on this page, then try to find others at home.

short-tail lizard

long-tail lizard

A super heroine can fly off quickly in a short cape.

A king walks slowly in a long cloak.

Here is a short line of elephants waiting for a bus.

The bus has not arrived yet and the short line has become a long one.

Short socks cover my ankles.

Long socks almost reach my knees.

If you had a choice of long, slurpy spaghetti strands or short pasta bows, which would you want to eat?

Try this! Make a slinky snake

1. Get nine paper cups and paint them.

2. Take a cup for the head. Stick an eye on it.

3. Using a pencil, carefully make a hole in the bottom of the cup.

4. Thread string through the hole and tie a knot.

5. Join the cups together with paper fasteners.

Pull your slinky snake along.

Most cats have long tails, but the Manx cat has a short, stubby one.

looooong neck

If my neck was as long as a giraffe's, I could see high above the trees.

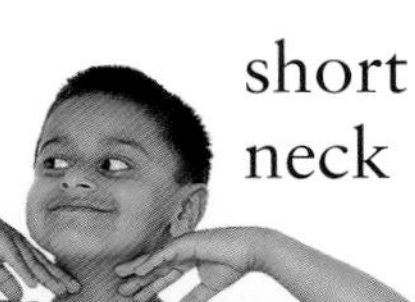

short neck

Did you know?

The giraffe's neck is longer than any other animal's.

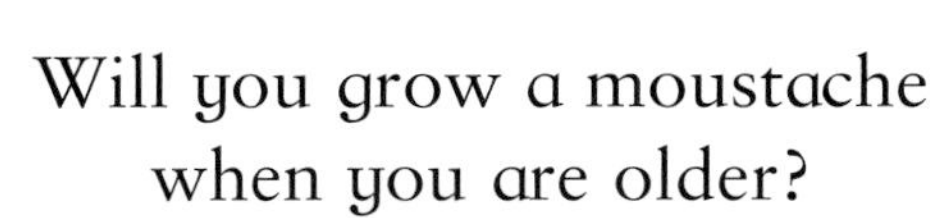

Will you grow a moustache when you are older?

Will your hair be long or short?

Thick and thin

Would you choose the thick or thin things on this page? Is one better than the other?

Help yourself to a piece of cake. Which slice would you like?

Two monkeys are swinging on ropes.

Which rope do you think will break?

Did you know?

Polar bears have thick fur coats to keep them warm in the cold.

The teddy bear's book is thinner. A quick read!

The wizard's thick book of magic is full of weird and wonderful spells!

How shall I wear my hair . . .

Which spiders have the thickest legs?

A thick sweater warms you up on cold days.

A thin T-shirt keeps you cool on hot days.

This frog and squirrel are painting.

Are their paintings the same?

A thick rubber ring will help you to float in water.

Can you spin a hula-hoop around your waist?

Would you rather munch on a very thick sandwich or a very thin one?

Try this!

Thick and thin sandwiches

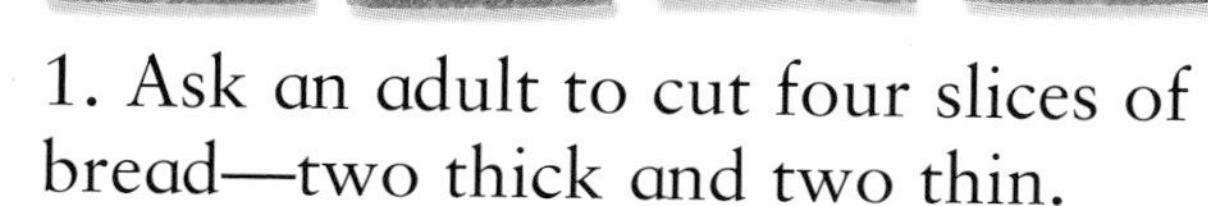

1. Ask an adult to cut four slices of bread—two thick and two thin. Butter them.
2. Ask for two slices of cheese—one thick and one thin.
3. Now ask for four slices of cucumber—two thick and two thin.
4. Make one very thick and one very thin sandwich.

thick sandwich

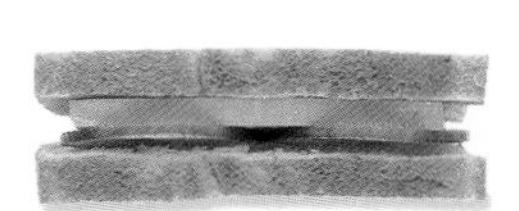

thin sandwich

Tall and short

There are tall and short things all around us. Which ones are taller or shorter than you?

Are you taller than your teddy bear?

Which of these towers has more beakers?

We need a taller ladder to rescue the chicken from the tower. This short ladder will not reach to the top.

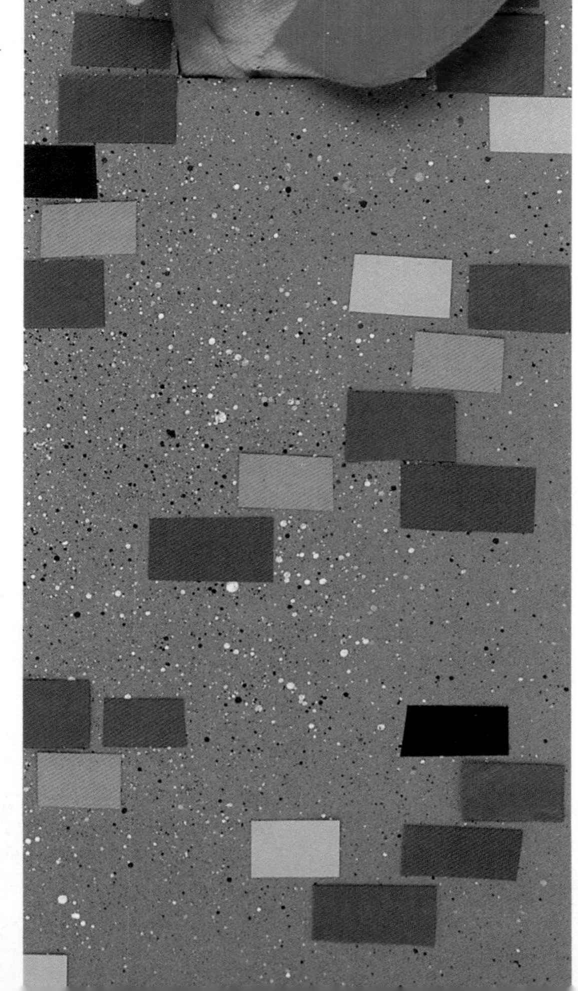

Dessert is a delicious treat. Which one would you choose to eat?

Try this! Who wears a hat?

1.Think of two people who wear hats. Draw them on a piece of paper.

2. Now think about their hats. Are they tall or short? Draw them on the picture.

3. Color in your pictures with felt-tip pens or crayons.

Pull out the sides of a trick mirror and it will make you look short. Push in on the sides and you will look taller.

Look at these two teddy bear towers. Which one is taller?

Can you find any differences between these two hats?

a tall blade of grass

a short one

Wide and narrow

Deciding whether things are wide or narrow is a way of seeing how much space they take up.

wide tie   narrow tie

Stretching out to walk through a wide gap.

Squeezing through a narrow gap.

A mouse hole is wide enough for a tiny mouse but too narrow for a fat cat!

Which is the wide boat and which is the narrower boat?

wide blue sea

A big car needs four wide tires.

A skinny bike only needs two narrow tires.

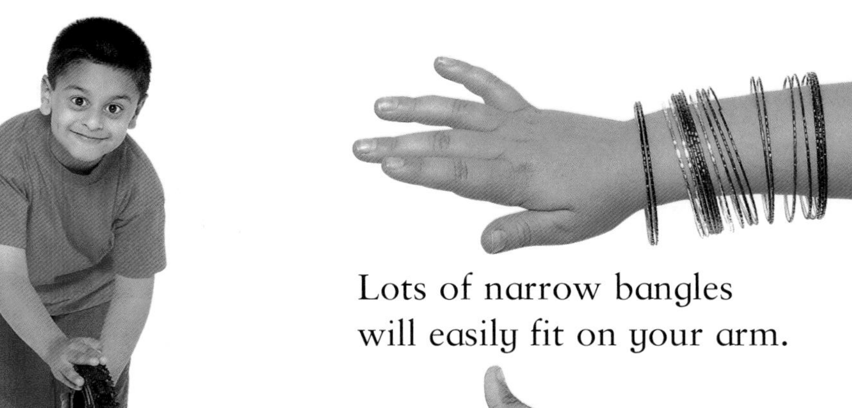

Lots of narrow bangles will easily fit on your arm.

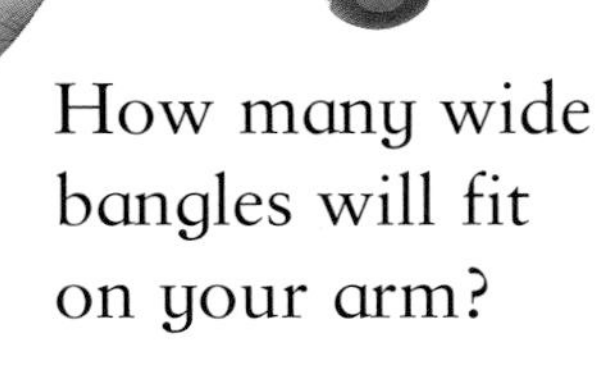

How many wide bangles will fit on your arm?

Two elephants wobbling along a narrow tightrope. Are they going to make it across?

Spiders scuttle along a wide plank.

Some ribbons are wide and silky. Others are narrow and fine.

Would you choose to wear . . .

narrow, clingy leggings . . .

or wide, baggy pants?

For an eye-popping finale, . . . stretch your arms out as far as you can.

The same size

Two socks, two shoes, two gloves—when two things are the same size, we say that they make a pair.

Two shoes in the same size make a pair.

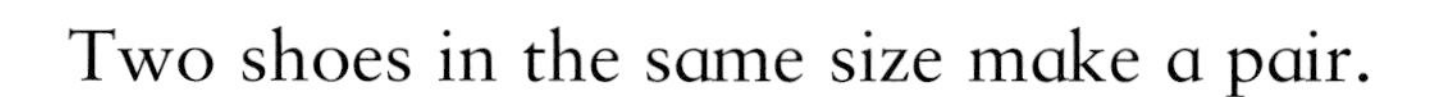

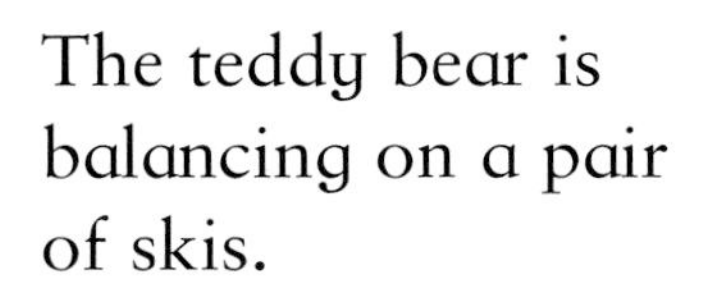

The teddy bear is balancing on a pair of skis.

Now he can slide down the snowy mountain slope.

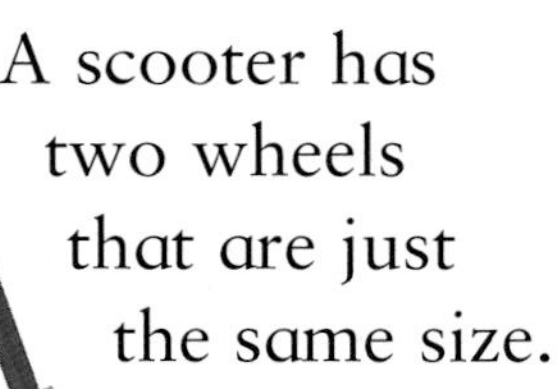

A scooter has two wheels that are just the same size.

Make sure that your roller skates are the same size!

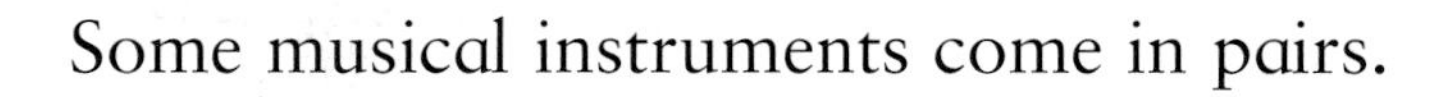

Some musical instruments come in pairs.

You need two cymbals to make a loud noise.

Shake your maracas gently for a soft sound or hard for a loud one.

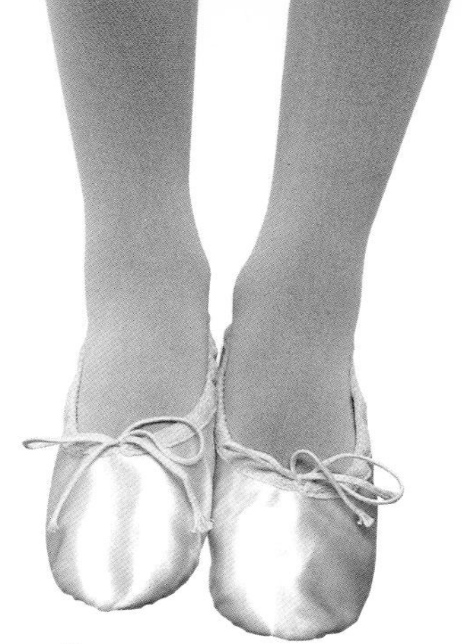

Whose shoes?

A pair of shoes that curl at the end. Who can they belong to?

glittery dancing shoes

A perfect fit! The prince has finally found his princess.

Two cold hands need two wool gloves.

Do you think these gloves will fit?

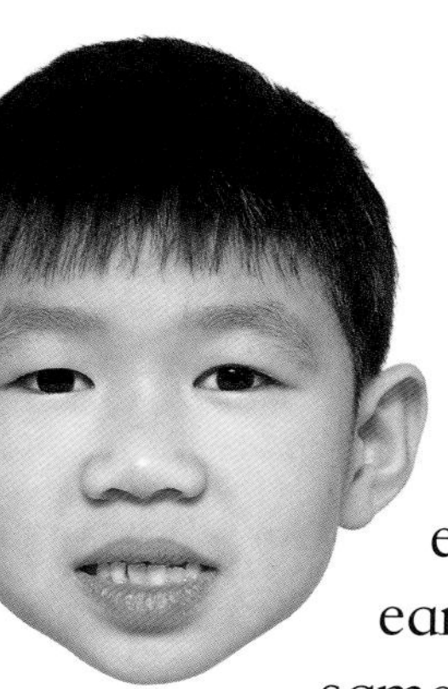

Look at yourself closely in the mirror.

You have two eyes and two ears just the same size.

What other parts of your body are the same size?

Did you know?

Your back relaxes and stretches out while you are sleeping at night. So when you wake-up you are a little bit taller than you were the day before.

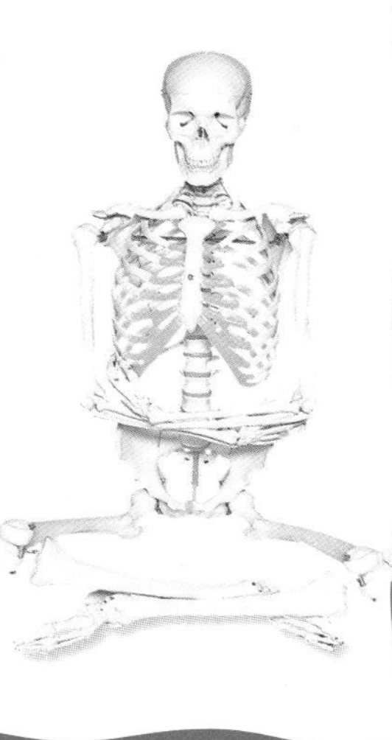

Right size, wrong size

Are these children wearing the right-size clothes?

It's important to have some things just the right size. You cannot ride a bike that is much too big, or wear shoes that are too small.

This chair is the right size.

Oops this one isn't.

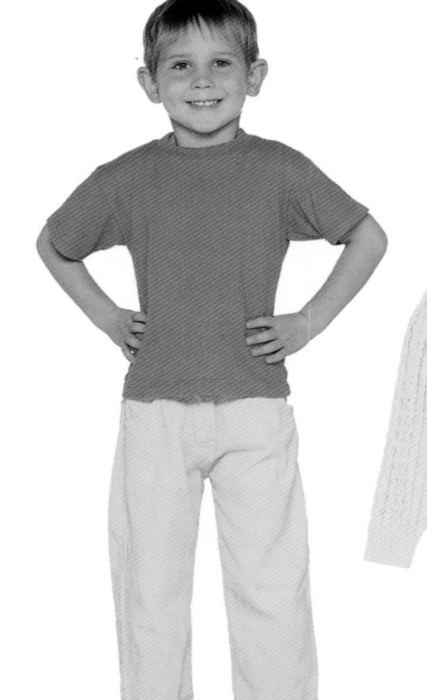

Try this!

Make a paper doll

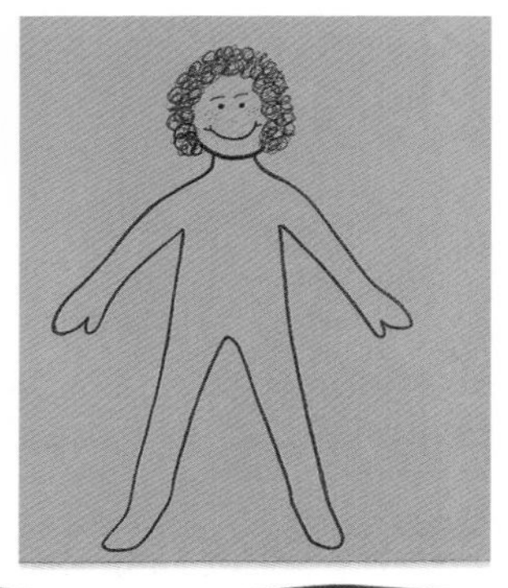

1. Draw a paper doll. It can be anything you want—an animal or a girl or a boy.

2. Lay see-through paper over the drawing. Draw some clothes for the doll.

3. Cut out the clothes and stick them on the doll. Do they fit?

Can you eat a big piece of cake in just one bite?

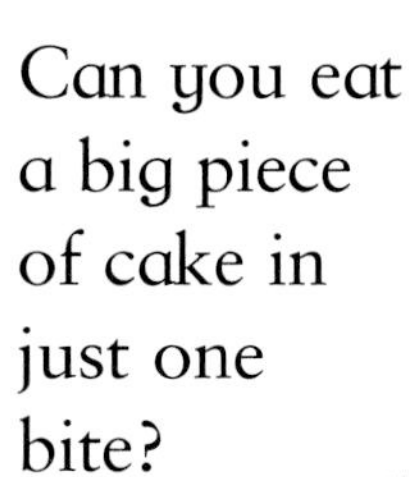

A small mouthful of cheese is almost right.

A piece of popcorn is just the right size.

These shoes are the wrong size for me . . .

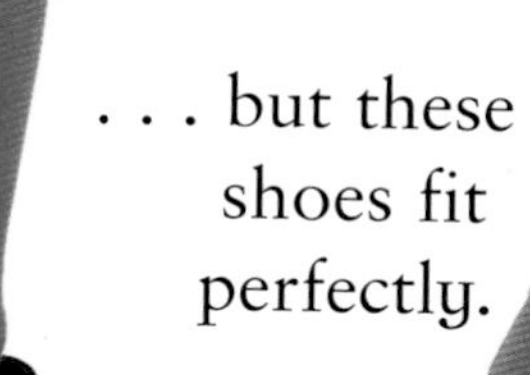

. . . but these shoes fit perfectly.

Did you know?

You need to be measured to know which clothes and shoes are the right size for you.

Two teddy bears are going for a ride.

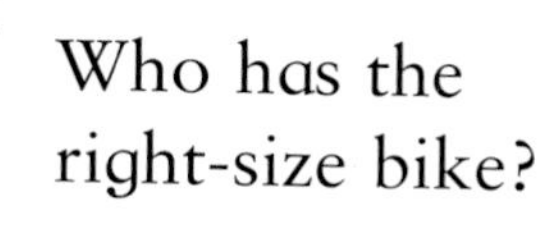

Who has the right-size bike?

Are these suitcases the right size?

too big

too small

the wrong-size toothbrush

Who is wearing the wrong-size glasses?

the right-size toothbrush

GROWING UP

Our body changes as we get older. We grow taller and wider and we need bigger and bigger things.

A one-year-old baby can crawl.

A three-year-old toddler can walk and run.

An eight-year-old child can do things f-a-s-t!

Babies grow out of their clothes very quickly.

Toddlers learn how to dress themselves.

A bigger child needs bigger clothes.

A baby wears slippers to keep its feet warm.

A toddler's shoes slip on and off easily.

How old were you when you first tied your shoelaces?

Some babies are carried in baby seats like this.

How old do you think the owner of this tricycle is?

Training wheels will help you when you learn to ride a bike.

A 13-year-old teenager is tall and strong.

At 25, you may have stopped growing!

Whose shirt is this?

Do you like to wear fashionable clothes?

Sneakers are comfortable and easy to walk in.

High-heeled shoes are harder to walk in.

Try this!

See how you grow

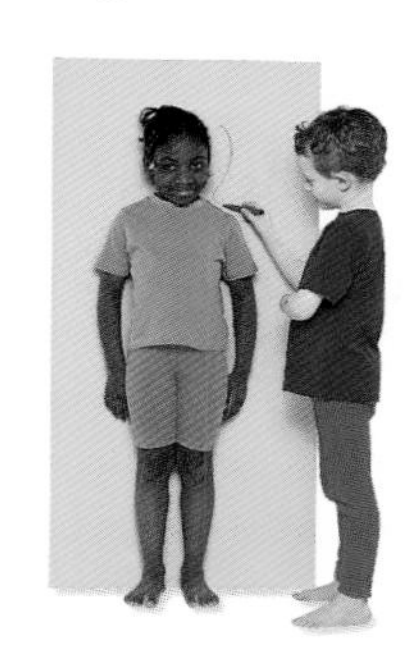

1. Hang a big piece of paper on the wall. Stand in front of it and ask a friend to draw around you.

2. When you step away from the paper, the drawing will show the shape of your body.

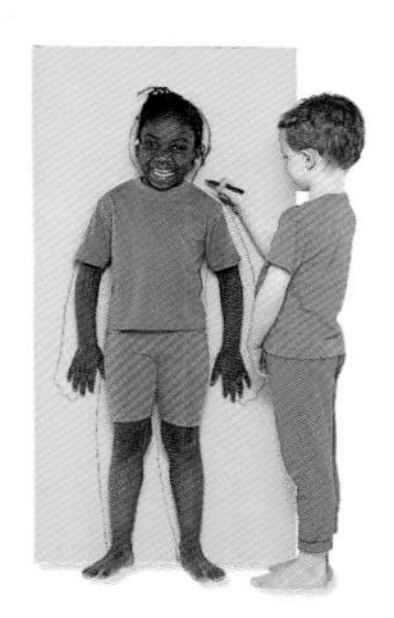

3. Do the same thing one month later. Ask your friend to draw around you in a different color.

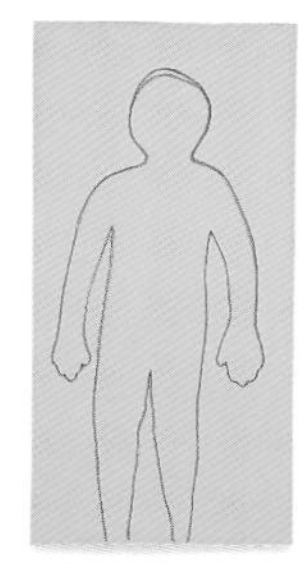

4. Take a ruler and measure the difference between the two body shapes. Have you grown?

When you are older, you can ride on the road.

Only adults are allowed to ride motorcycles.

Watch plants grow...

Plants and animals are living things, too. Like people, they start life small but, as long as they have plenty of food, they soon begin to grow.

Small acorns grow on oak trees.

They fall to the ground in autumn and grow in the spring.

The young tree grows leaves in its first year.

20 years later, the oak tree is as tall as a house, and still growing!

Try this! Grow some sprouts

1. Soak some mung beans in water overnight. Drain them and leave in a covered jar.

2. After two days, the beans will start to sprout. Sprinkle them on top of a delicious salad.

Watch animals grow...

Baby animals grow more quickly than humans. In just a couple of months, they may be ten times bigger than when they were born.

When kittens are born, their mother licks them clean.

Even after one week a kitten's eyes are still tightly closed.

At three weeks, the kitten has started to move around. But it is still not very strong.

Nine weeks old, and the kitten is almost ready for its first trip outside.

This puppy is three days old. It only sleeps and eats.

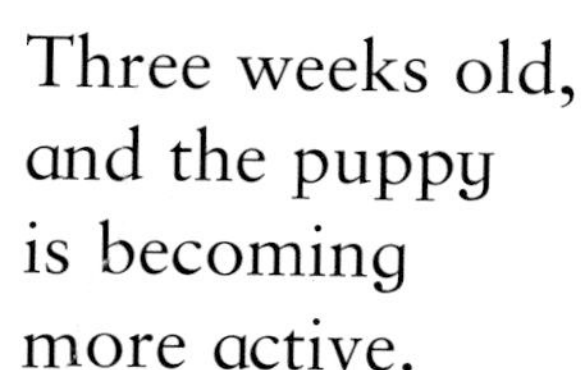

Three weeks old, and the puppy is becoming more active.

At five weeks, puppies begin to be curious about the world around them.

After eight weeks the puppies are ready to go to a new home.

This baby owl is resting after hatching out of its shell.

A group of two-week-old owlets wait for a meal.

Four weeks old, and the owlets are moving around their nest.

After twelve weeks an owlet loses its fluffy feathers and is growing fast.

Life-size animals

Are we the smallest creatures on this page?

All the animals on this page are shown life-size. Are they bigger or smaller than your hand?

Soon this puss-moth caterpillar will turn into a gorgeous butterfly.

This duckling hatched just two days ago!

Are these baby mice smaller than your thumb?

This baby tortoise takes bigger steps every day.

This small kitten would look enormous to a tiny mouse!

Ladybugs crawl through the garden, eating bugs even smaller than them!

Watch out! A python is coming this way—and it's body is as long as a bus!

Snails have eyes at the end of their feelers. See how long the feelers are.

Tortoiseshell butterflies stretch out their wings to soak up the sun's rays.

A tarantula's legs are longer than a snail.

A guinea pig's whiskers are wider than its face.

Changing siZeS

How can you change the size of something? By stretching or shrinking it, or blowing it up, or breaking it into bits!

You can build a big castle with lots of little bricks.

Break a big bar of chocolate into little squares and share it with your friends.

My T-shirt is too small for me now. It must have shrunk in the wash.

Yum! Yum!

I am hungry.

Oh dear!

Now I am full.

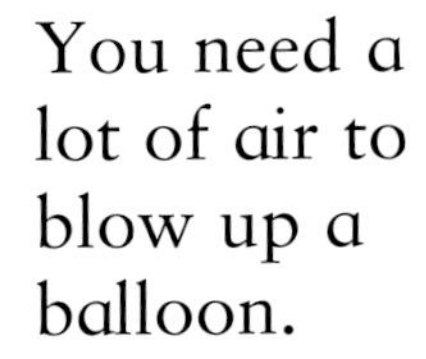

You need a lot of air to blow up a balloon.

Puff, puff! It is getting bigger.

Puff, puff! Now it is even bigger.

My skirt has an elastic waist. It fits me perfectly. Or it can stretch and stretch to make room for two.

A small amount of cake batter becomes a big cake after it is cooked.

Can you put all the pieces of a jigsaw puzzle together?

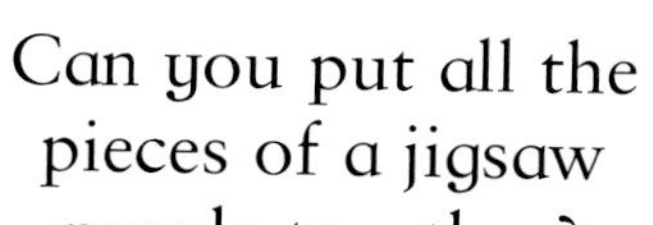

Now it is the same size as when I started.

Try this!

Make a picture puzzle

1. Draw a picture on a piece of heavy paper. Color it brightly.

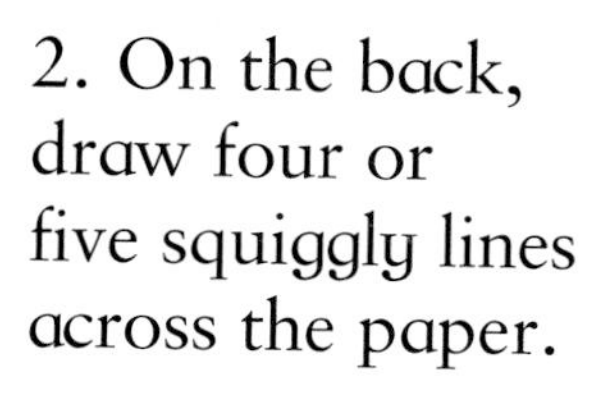

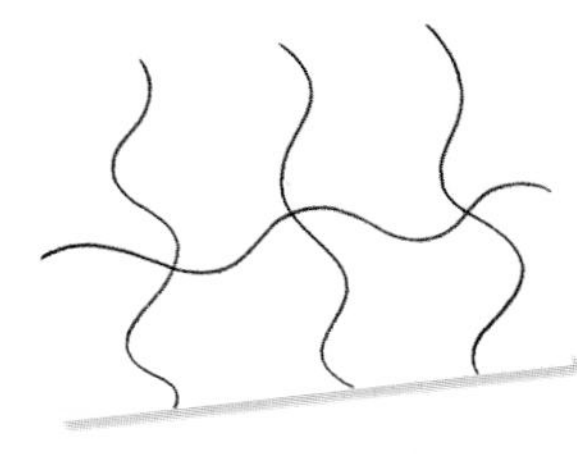

2. On the back, draw four or five squiggly lines across the paper.

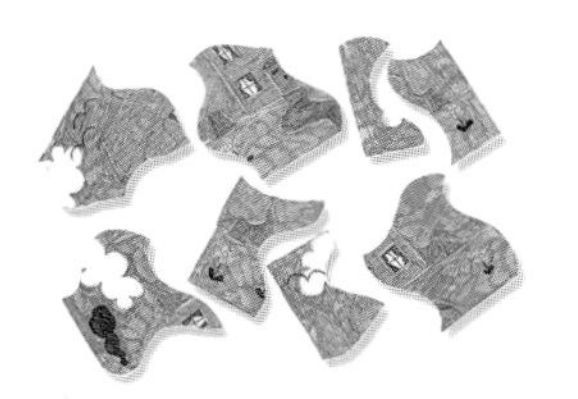

3. Cut the paper along the lines.

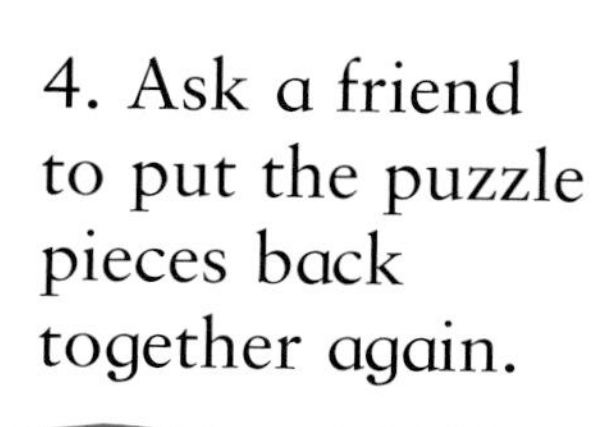

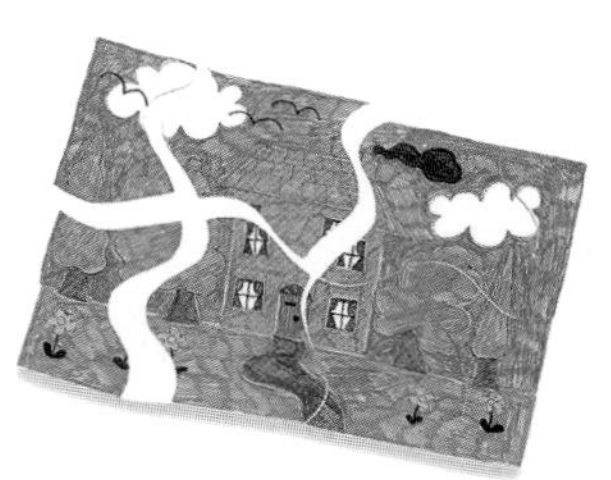

4. Ask a friend to put the puzzle pieces back together again.

Find the size

Take it in turns to throw the dice and move your marker around the board. When you land on a square, look for the answers on the page. You have ten seconds to do this. If you can't, you miss a turn. If you can, you have another turn. The first one to finish is the winner.

You will need 2 markers or buttons, a timer and a die.

START

4

I've got thin legs. Find the spider with thicker legs.

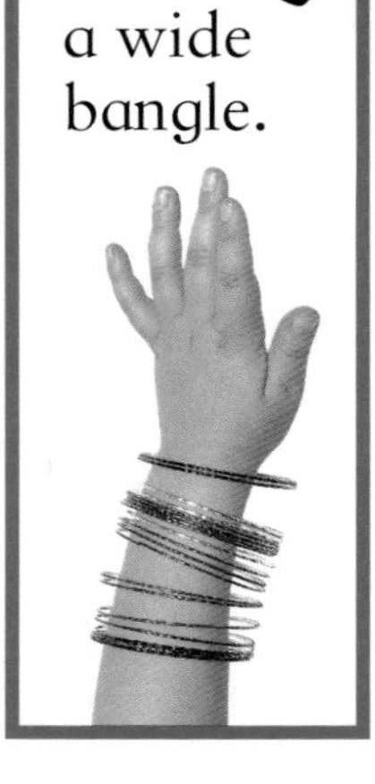

13

Find a shorter tower.

14

Find a longer blade of grass.

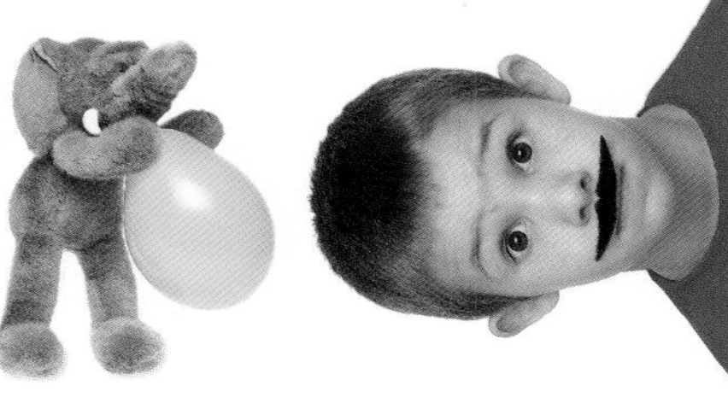

15

I was thinner before I ate that cheese. Where is the thinner me?

16

Find a narrower boat.

11

Find a thicker sandwich.

12

Find the same size boot.

17

Find an older kitten.

FINISH

18

Whoops! The elephant has sat on the wrong chair. Find the right-sized chair for him.

19

Find the wrong-sized toothbrush.

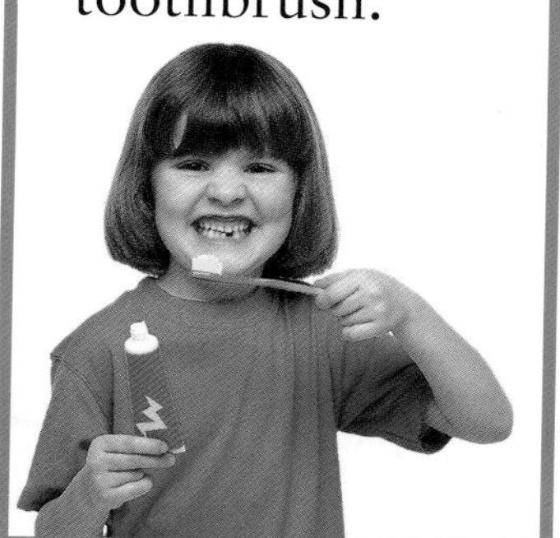

20

These shoes are too big—find me a pair that will fit properly.

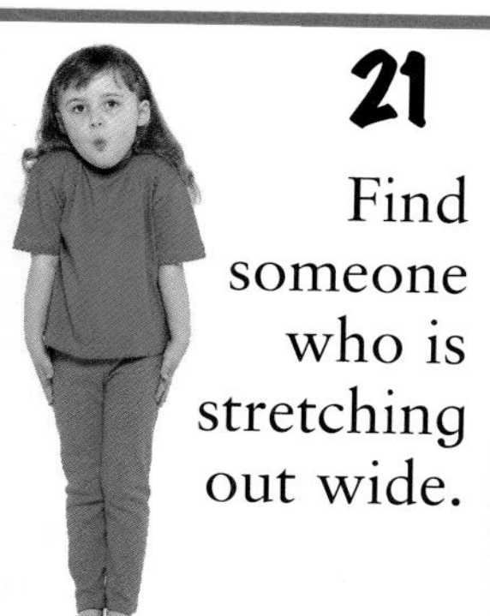

21

Find someone who is stretching out wide.

First published in 2000 by Lorenz Books

LORENZ BOOKS are available for bulk purchase for sales promotion and for
premium use. For details, write or call the sales director,
Lorenz Books, 27 West 20th Street, New York, NY 10011
(800) 354-9657

Lorenz Books is an imprint of
Anness Publishing Inc.

Publisher: Joanna Lorenz
Managing Editor, Children's Books: Gilly Cameron-Cooper
Project Editor: Joanne Hanks
Production Controller: Don Campaniello
Educational Consultant: Naima Browne
Design: Tessa Barwick
Photography: John Freeman
Stylist: Melanie Williams

The Publishers would like to thank the following children for modeling in this book:
Harriet Bartholomew, Jonathan Bartholomew, Daisy Bartlett,
Andrew Brown, April Cain, Milo Clare, Alice Crawley, Luke Fry,
Africa George, Safari George, Zaafir Ghany, Miriam Nadia Halgane,
Jackson Harrington, Madison Harrington, Faye Harrison, Jasmine Haynes,
Joseph Haynes, Rhys Hillier, Kadeem Johnson, Zamour Johnson, Sumaya Khassal,
Otis Lindblom Smith, Holly Matthews, Rebekah Murrell,
Lucie Ozanne-Martin, Philip Quach, Tom Rawlings, Grace Updon, James Xu

1 3 5 7 9 10 8 6 4 2